by Cathy Baker

CONTENTS

Introduction

Look over the wood furniture projects in this bulletin. See something you need? Here's a surprise for you. You don't need a basement full of power tools to build them. Just the simple hand tools listed below.

And you don't have to be a master carpenter, either. Just follow the step-by-step instructions and the illustrations. It's simple.

Tools

Hammer	Crosscut saw, back saw
Coping saw	Pencil
Measuring tape	Try-square
Smooth or block plane	Router plane
Chisel	Screw driver
Two C-clamps	Brace or hand drill

Drill bits, numbered $\frac{1}{8}$, $\frac{9}{64}$, $\frac{7}{32}$, $\frac{3}{8}$, $\frac{1}{4}$, $\frac{23}{64}$, $\frac{5}{16}$, $\frac{1}{2}$, $\frac{5}{8}$, and 1 inch

Whenever there is a common stock name of the measure of an article, it will be given in parentheses after the listing of the actual measurement of that article. For example, a piece of wood with the thickness of one and one-half inches is commonly called a two-by-four. If you ask for an article by its common stock name, you will save time and avoid confusion.

Wall Shelf

Need a place for those little breakable items you've collected, or those spice jars? Here it is, and it's a snap to build.

Bill of Materials

		Dimensions:		
Pieces	Use	thickness	width	length
2	sides	⅝"	7"	27½"
1	top	½"	7"	10"
1	upper shelf	½"	5"	10"
1	middle shelf	½"	6"	10"
1	lower shelf	½"	7"	10"

4-penny finish nails
cardboard for patterns

fig. 1

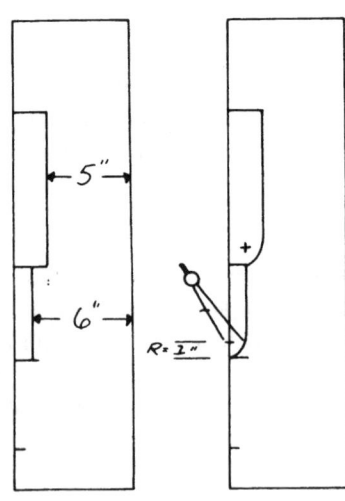

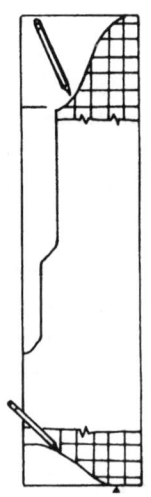

Procedure

1. Cut, plane and square the boards to the sizes given in the Bill of Materials.

2. Make a full-sized cardboard pattern of the shelf side. Lay it out on the boards as shown in *fig. 1.*

3. Saw the sides to shape with a coping saw. Start with the upper curve, then saw the two middle curves and finish with the lower end.

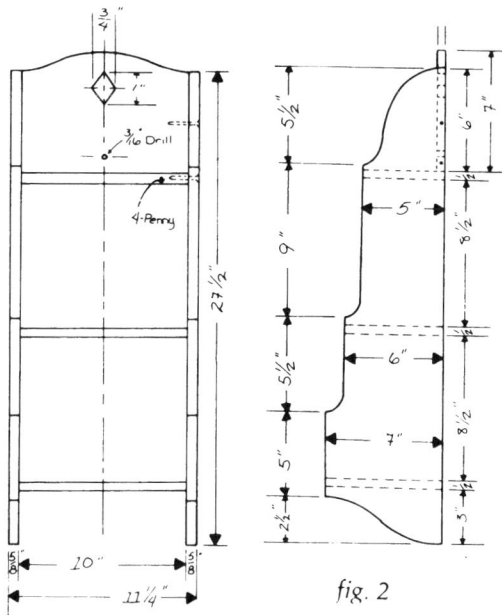

fig. 2

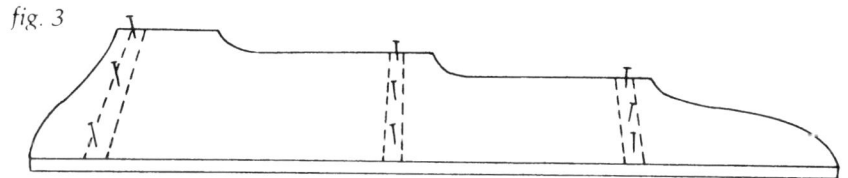

fig. 3

4. Sand all rough surfaces.

5. On both surfaces of the sides, draw two light lines where each shelf is to be fastened. Refer to the side view of *fig. 2.*

6. Start the nails through the outside of the shelf side until the points just come through on the inside. *fig. 3.*

7. Press the first shelf against the nail points. *fig. 4.*

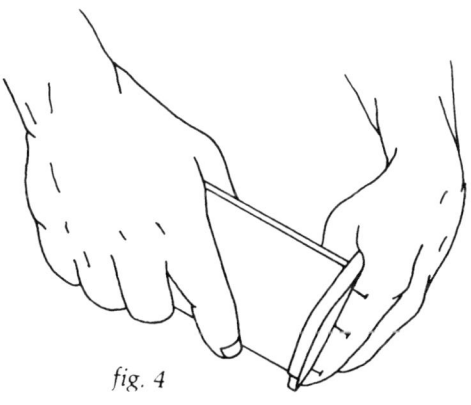

fig. 4

8. Brace the opposite end of the shelf against a flat area and drive in the nails. *fig. 5.* Continue in this manner with the other shelves.

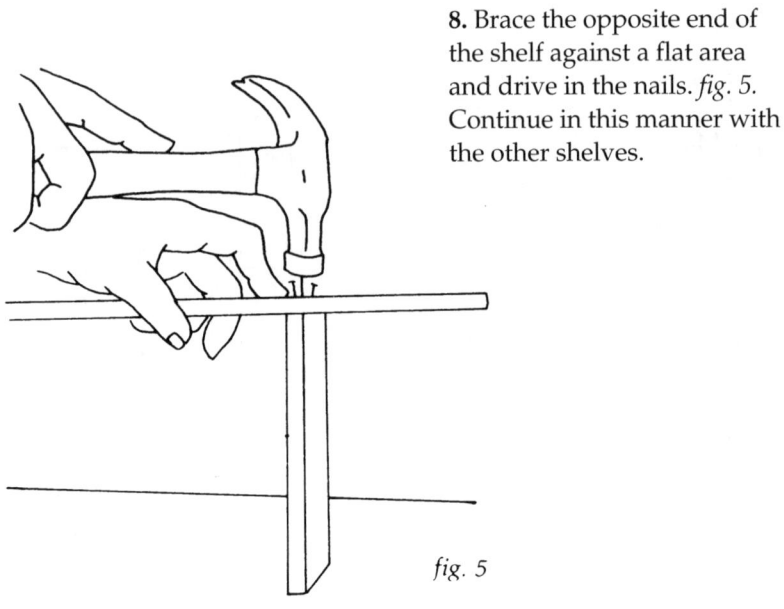

fig. 5

fig. 6

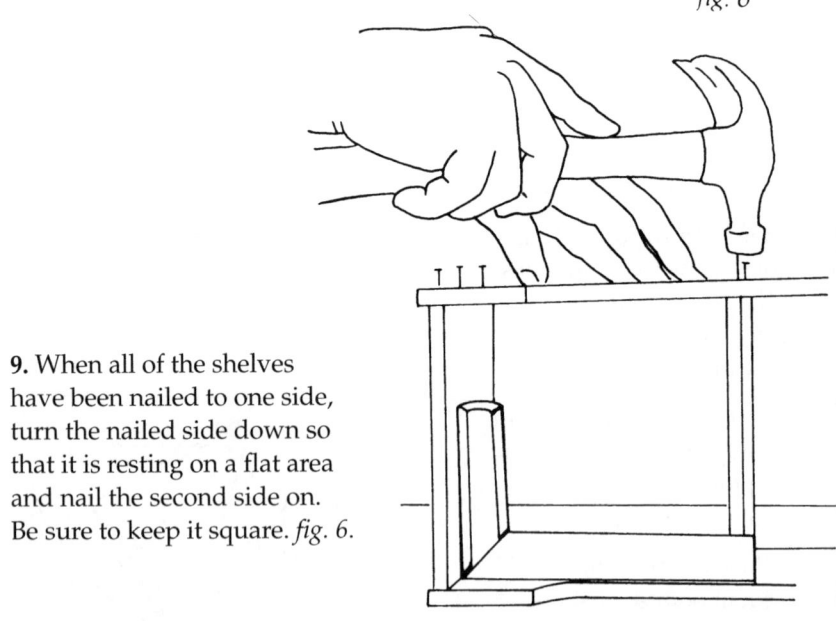

9. When all of the shelves have been nailed to one side, turn the nailed side down so that it is resting on a flat area and nail the second side on. Be sure to keep it square. *fig. 6.*

10. Make a pattern for the top piece as shown in *fig. 7*. Lay it out and saw to shape.

11. Drill a hole in the diamond, insert the coping blade, and saw the diamond to shape. Sand. Refer to *fig. 2*.

12. Nail the top to the sides and top shelf.

13. Do a final sanding and paint, stain, or varnish your shelf.

Top of Sides

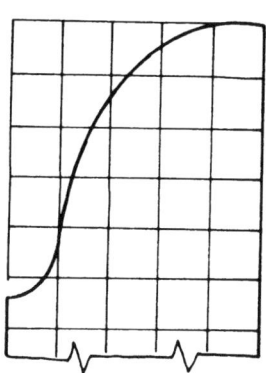

Top Piece

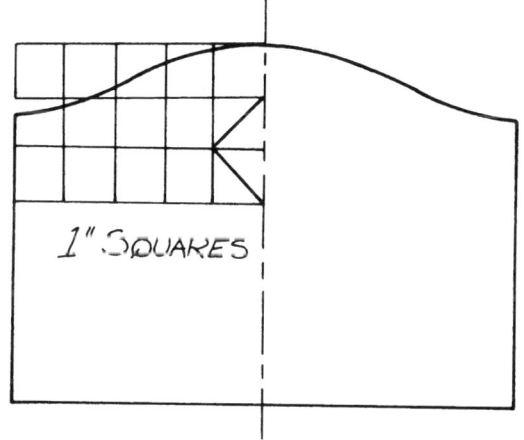

Patterns

fig. 7

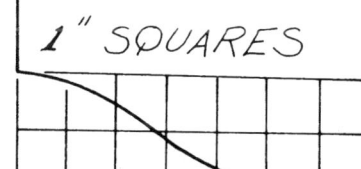

Bottom of Sides

-5-

Small Bench

*Or call it a side table if that's
what you need. It's sturdy,
handy, and decorative.*

Bill of Materials

Pieces	Use			
		Dimensions:		
		thickness	**width**	**length**
2	seat	1½"	5½"	18" (2 × 6)
2	rails	1½"	1½"	9¼" (2 × 2)
4	legs	1½"	2¾"	21" (2 × 3)
1	dowel	⅝" round × 17¼" long		

8-penny finishing nails
8 2" #8 flat-head screws

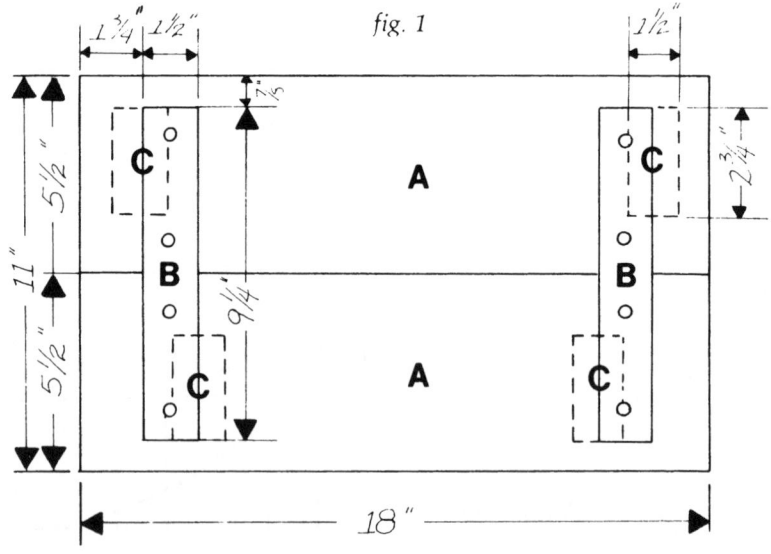

fig. 1

Procedure

1. Cut all stock to the sizes given in the Bill of Materials.

2. Nail the rails (B) to the underside of the seat pieces (A), as shown in *fig. 1.*

3. Lay out and cut the parallel angles on the ends of each leg. The finished length of each leg should be 18½". *fig. 2.*

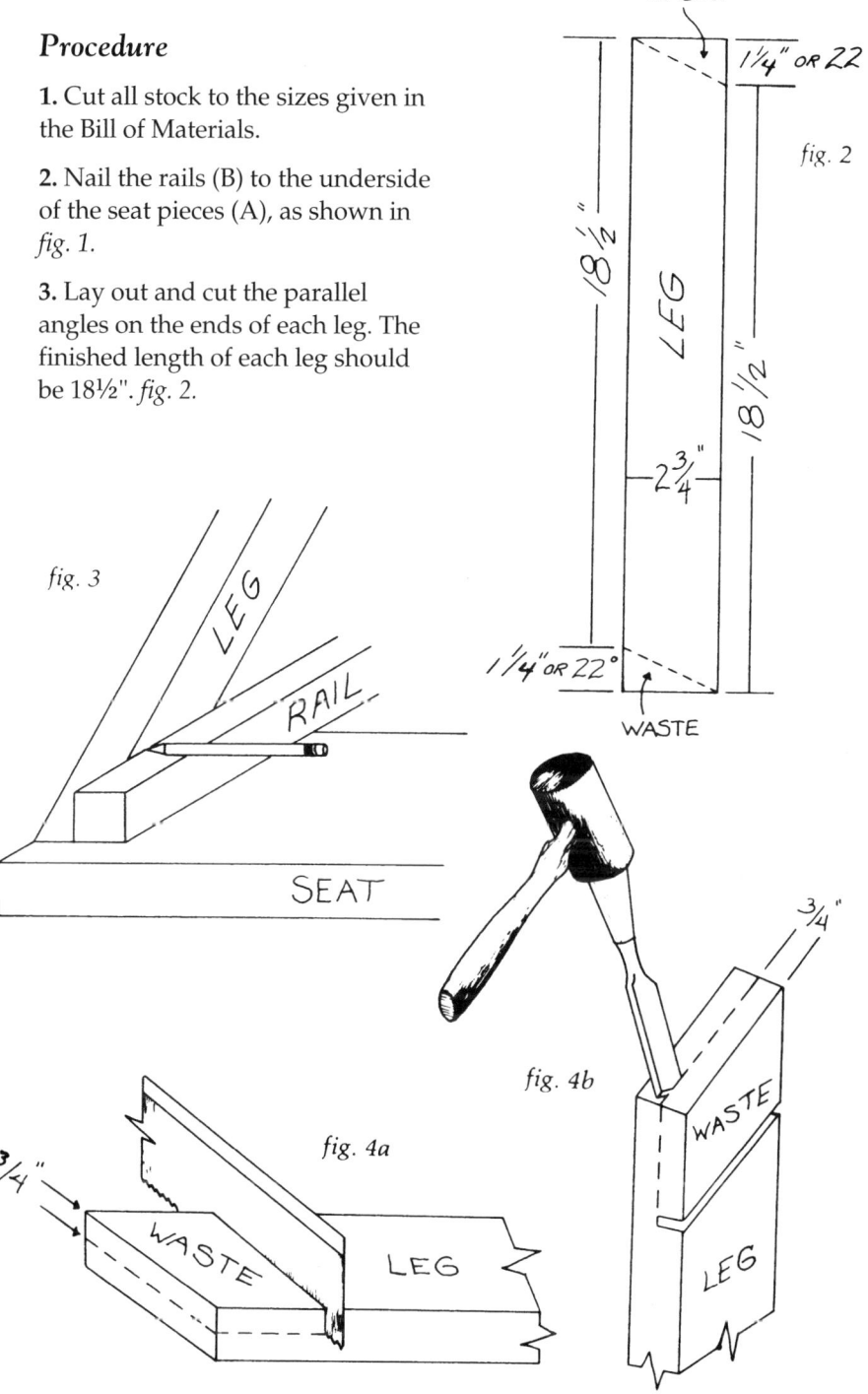

fig. 2

fig. 3

fig. 4a

fig. 4b

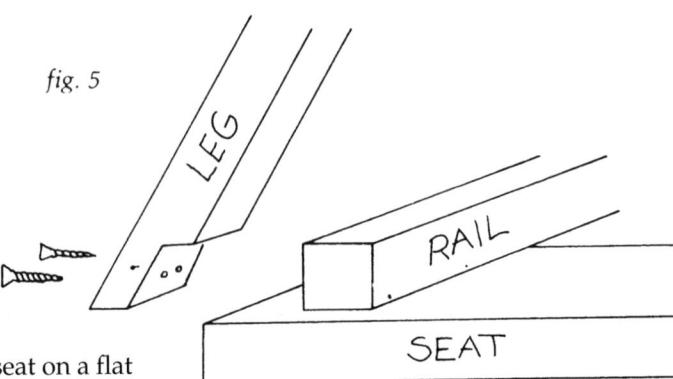

fig. 5

LEG

RAIL

SEAT

4. Place the seat on a flat area bottom side up. The rails will be exposed.

5. Lay out the rabbet joints at the tops of the legs. Hold each leg in place in turn. Placement may be determined by the dotted lines, marked **C,** in *fig. 1.* Draw a line along the leg where the top of the leg meets the side. *fig. 3.*

6. Cut the rabbet joint. Cut into the leg ¾ of an inch along the drawn line. Chisel out the waste. *fig. 4.*

7. After making trial assemblies of the legs, drill starter holes for the screws and attach the legs to the rails. *fig. 5.*

8. Drill ⅝" holes through the center of the cross formed by the legs. Be sure they are in the same position on both sides.

9. Pound the dowel through the holes. *fig. 6.*

10. Sand the bench.

11. This project may be stained or painted.

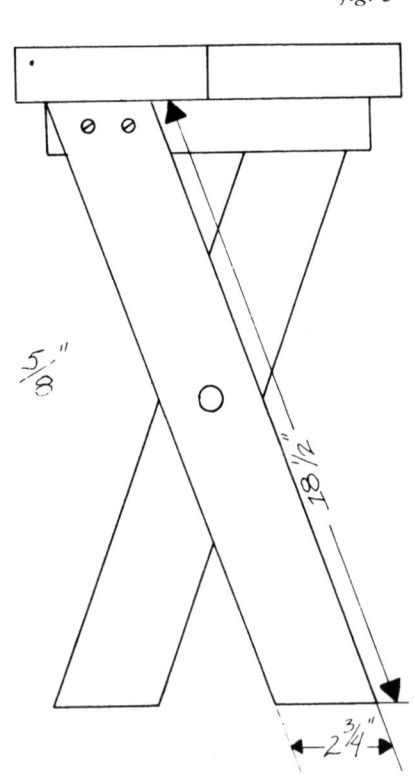

fig. 6

$5\frac{\scriptstyle 1}{\scriptstyle 8}$"

$18\frac{\scriptstyle 1}{\scriptstyle 2}$"

$2\frac{\scriptstyle 3}{\scriptstyle 4}$"

Picnic Table and Benches

Just the thing for your backyard meals on summer evenings. The whole family will praise the carpenter who builds these and join him or her in using them.

Bill of Materials

Picnic Table

		Dimensions:		
Pieces	Use	thickness	width	length
5	table top	1½"	5½"	70" (2 × 6)
3	rails	1½"	2½"	25" (2 × 3)
4	legs	1½"	3½"	36" (2 × 4)
2	braces	1½"	2½"	21½" (2 × 3)

16   ¼" × 3½" round-head carriage bolts, nuts

10   ³⁄₁₆" washers and

6   ⅝" washers

7   2½" #8 wood screws

Two Benches

Pieces	Use	Dimensions: thickness	width	length
4	bench top	1½"	5½"	70" (2 × 6)
6	rails	1½"	2½"	10" (2 × 3)
8	legs	1½"	3½"	18½" (2 × 4)
4	braces	1½"	2½"	12" (2 × 3)

20 ¼" × 3½" round-head carriage bolts and nuts

8 ³⁄₁₆" washers

12 ⅝" washers

8 2½" #8 screws

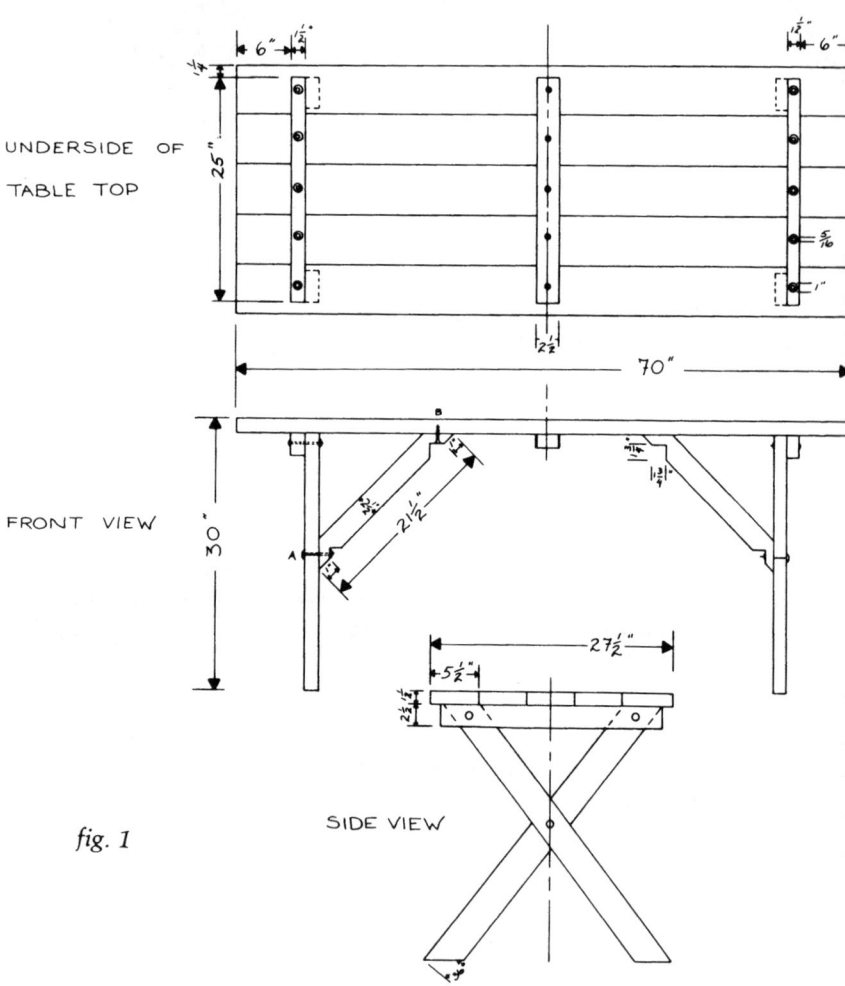

UNDERSIDE OF TABLE TOP

FRONT VIEW

SIDE VIEW

fig. 1

Procedure for Both

1. Cut all stock to the sizes given in the Bill of Materials.

2. Cut the parallel angles on the legs. These angles are laid out and cut in the same manner as they were with the Small Bench. The angle used for the table legs is 36°, or measure 2½" down the leg from the corners on alternate sides and cut diagonally across from the opposite corner. The angle for the bench legs is 22°, the same as for the Small Bench. Refer to *fig. 2* of the Small Bench project on page 6.

3. Cut the 45° angles on the braces. These are opposite angles. Measure down 2½" from the corners on the same sides and cut diagonally across from the opposite corners. See the front view in *fig. 1.*

4. Cut the notches on the braces. Refer to the front view in *fig. 1.*

5. Lay all of the top pieces side-by-side on a level area. Be sure that they are square. See the underside view in *fig. 1.*

6. Put the rails in position. See the underside view in *fig. 1.* The rails are put in the same place on the bench.

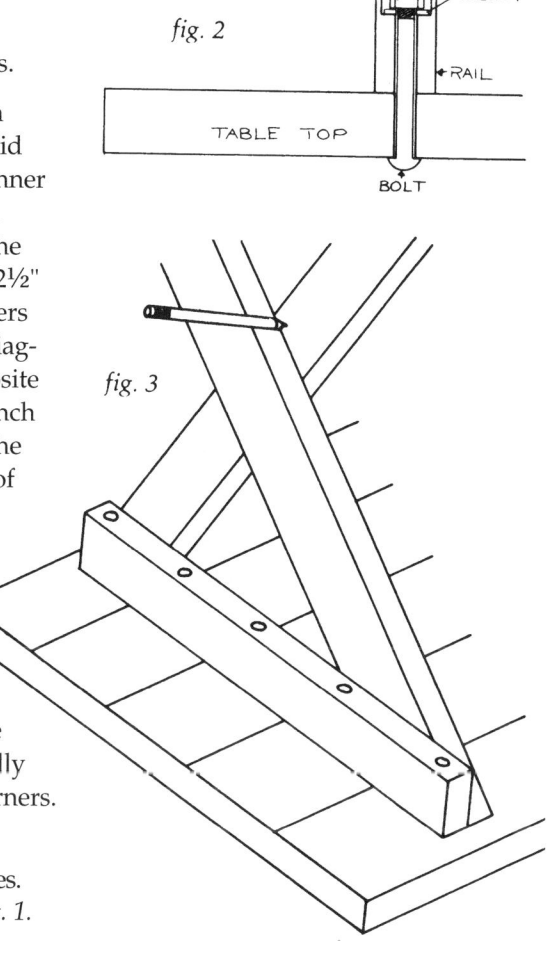

fig. 2

NUT · WASHER · RAIL · TABLE TOP · BOLT

fig. 3

7. Clamp each end rail in place in turn and bore ⁵⁄₁₆" holes through the rail and table top or bench top for the bolts. From the top of the rail, as you look at it, widen the ⁵⁄₁₆" hole to 1 inch to a depth of ¾". Do this to each hole on the end rails. See the underside view in *fig. 1.* for placement and the detail view in *fig. 2.*

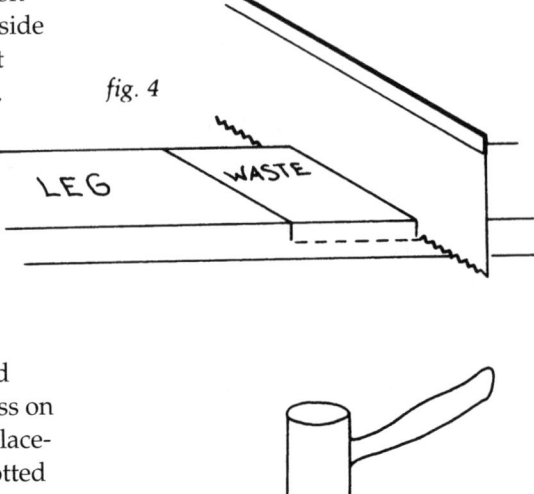

fig. 4

8. Bolt the end rails to the top.

9. Clamp the center rail. Drill holes in the center rail and screw it to the table top.

10. Put the legs in place and draw a line where they cross on each side of each leg. For placement of the legs, see the dotted lines in the underside view in *fig. 1.* Also refer to *fig. 3.*

11. Make a ¾" deep cut through each drawn line. Chisel out the waste. *fig. 4* and 5.

fig. 5

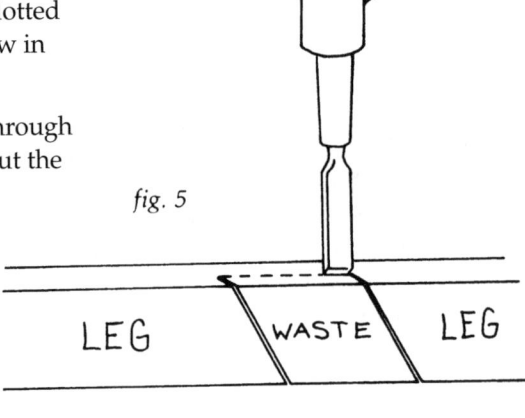

12. Fit the overlapping joints together and put the legs in place again. *fig. 5.*

13. Drill ⁵⁄₁₆" holes through the legs and rails for the bolts.

14. Bolt the legs to the rails. See the front view in *fig. 1.* For greater strength, these legs could be rabbeted to the rails as in the Small Bench project on page 6.

15. Put the brace in place and clamp it there. Bore a ⁵⁄₁₆" hole from the center of the notched area of the brace through to the outside of the overlapping joint. Bolt the joint to the brace. See

the area marked 'A' in the front view of *fig. 1.*

16. Drill a starter hole through the center of the second notch and part way through the table or bench top. Screw the brace to the table or bench top. See the section marked 'B' in the front view in *fig. 1.*

17. Sand the rough edges.

18. Paint or stain the project.

Adirondack Chair

Build this, then enjoy the fruits of your labors as you relax in comfort and deep satisfaction. Or build the double chair for his 'n' her enjoyment.

Bill of Materials

Single Chair

Pieces	Use	thickness	width	length
		Dimensions:		
2	front legs	¾"	3½"	20" (1 × 4)
2	slanted legs	¾"	3½"	30" (1 × 4)
1	triangles	1½"	3½"	6" (2 × 4)
1	front brace	¾"	3½"	22" (1 × 4)
1	back brace	¾"	2½"	22" (1 × 3)
1	arm brace	1½"	1½"	22" (2 × 2)
2	arms	¾"	5½"	27" (1 × 6)
2	back pieces	¾"	3½"	26" (1 × 4)
3	back pieces	¾"	3½"	28" (1 × 4)
1	front seat piece	¾"	5½"	22" (1 × 6)
3	seat pieces	¾"	3½"	22" (1 × 4)

1 box of 1½" #8 flat head screws
1 box of 1½" #15 brads

Double Chair

Pieces	Use	Dimensions: thickness	width	length
2	front legs	¾"	3½"	20" (1 × 4)
2	slanted legs	¾"	3½"	30" (1 × 4)
1	triangles	1½"	3½"	6" (2 × 4)
1	front brace	¾"	3½"	44" (1 × 4)
1	back brace	¾"	2½"	44" (1 × 3)
1	arm brace	1½"	1½"	44" (2 × 2)
2	arms	¾"	5½"	27" (1 × 6)
4	back pieces	¾"	3½"	26" (1 × 4)
6	back pieces	¾"	3½"	28" (1 × 4)
1	seat piece	¾"	5½"	44" (1 × 6)
3	seat pieces	¾"	3½"	44" (1 × 4)
1	center seat brace	¾"	3½"	14" (1 × 4)

1 box of 1½" #8 flat head screws
1 box of 1½" #15 brads

Procedure

1. Cut all stock to the lengths given in the Bill of Materials.

2. Make a diagonal cut across the 1½" × 3½" × 6" piece of stock so that it forms two triangles 3 ½" × 6" × 7". *fig. 1.*

3. Put the 6" face of each triangle against the front outside corner of each front leg. Drill starter holes and screw the triangle in place. *fig. 1.*

4. Cut the angles on the slanted legs. *fig. 2.*

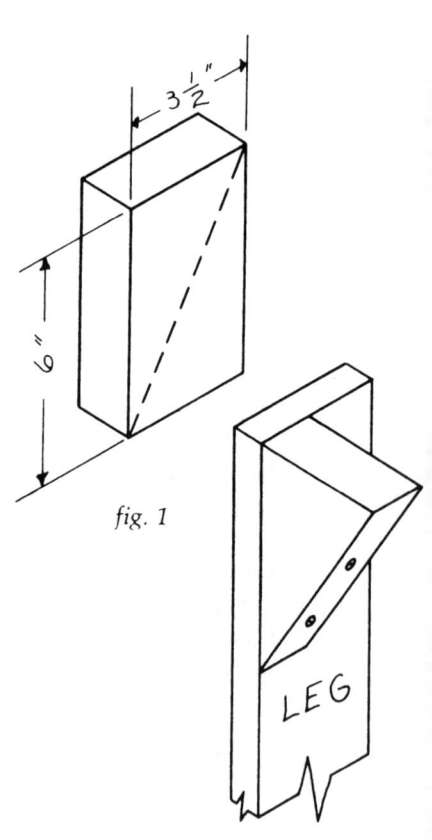

fig. 1

LEG

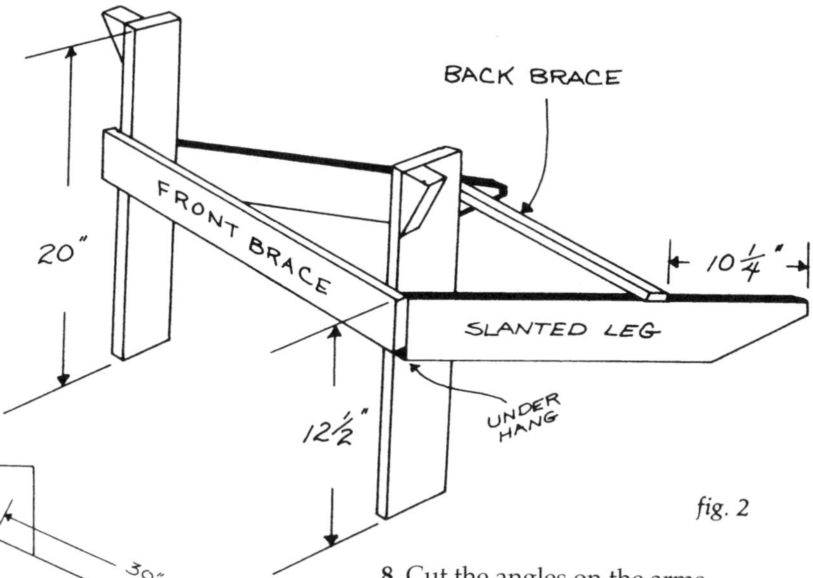

BACK BRACE

FRONT BRACE

20"

10 1/4"

SLANTED LEG

UNDER HANG

12 1/2"

fig. 2

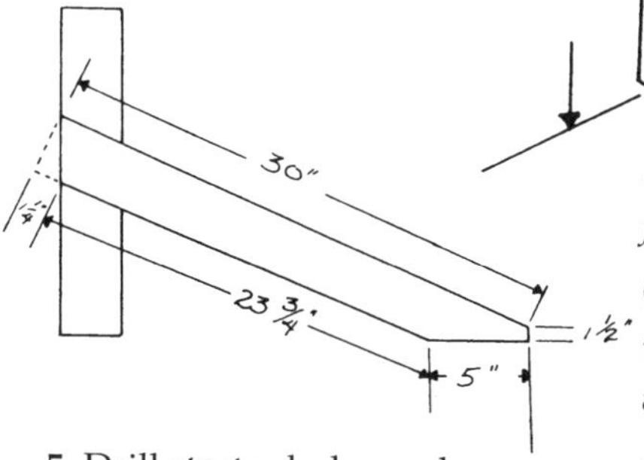

30"

23 3/4"

1/2"

5"

5. Drill starter holes and screw the slanted legs to the front legs. *fig. 2.*

6. Plane the corner of the back brace as shown in *fig. 3.*

7. Drill starter holes and screw the front and back braces in place. Refer to *fig. 2.*

8. Cut the angles on the arms. *fig. 4.*

9. Drill starter holes and screw the arm brace to the back of the arms. *fig. 4.*

10. Cut the angles on the back pieces. *fig. 5.*

11. Have someone hold the arm brace while you tack the arms to the front legs with the 1½" brads. *fig. 6.*

12. Tack the two outside back pieces in place. *fig. 6.*

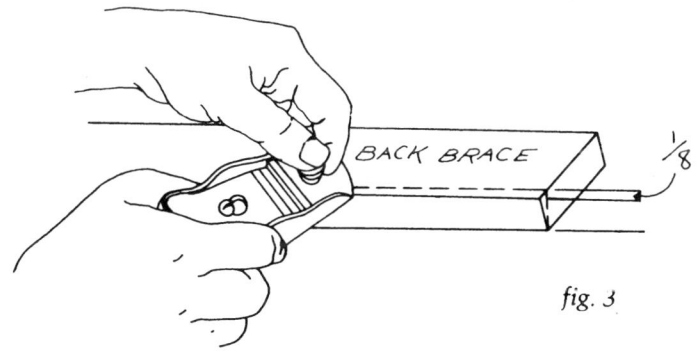

BACK BRACE

1/8

fig. 3

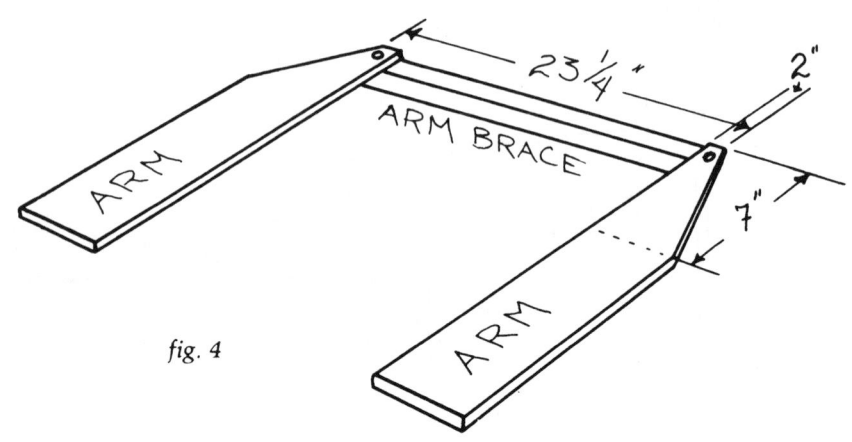

fig. 4

13. Drill starter holes and screw the arm to the triangles attached to the front legs. *fig. 6.*

14. Drill starter holes and fasten the two outside back pieces securely with the screws. Fasten the rest of the back pieces. Be sure that they are spaced evenly. *fig. 6.*

DOUBLE CHAIR

fig. 5

SINGLE CHAIR

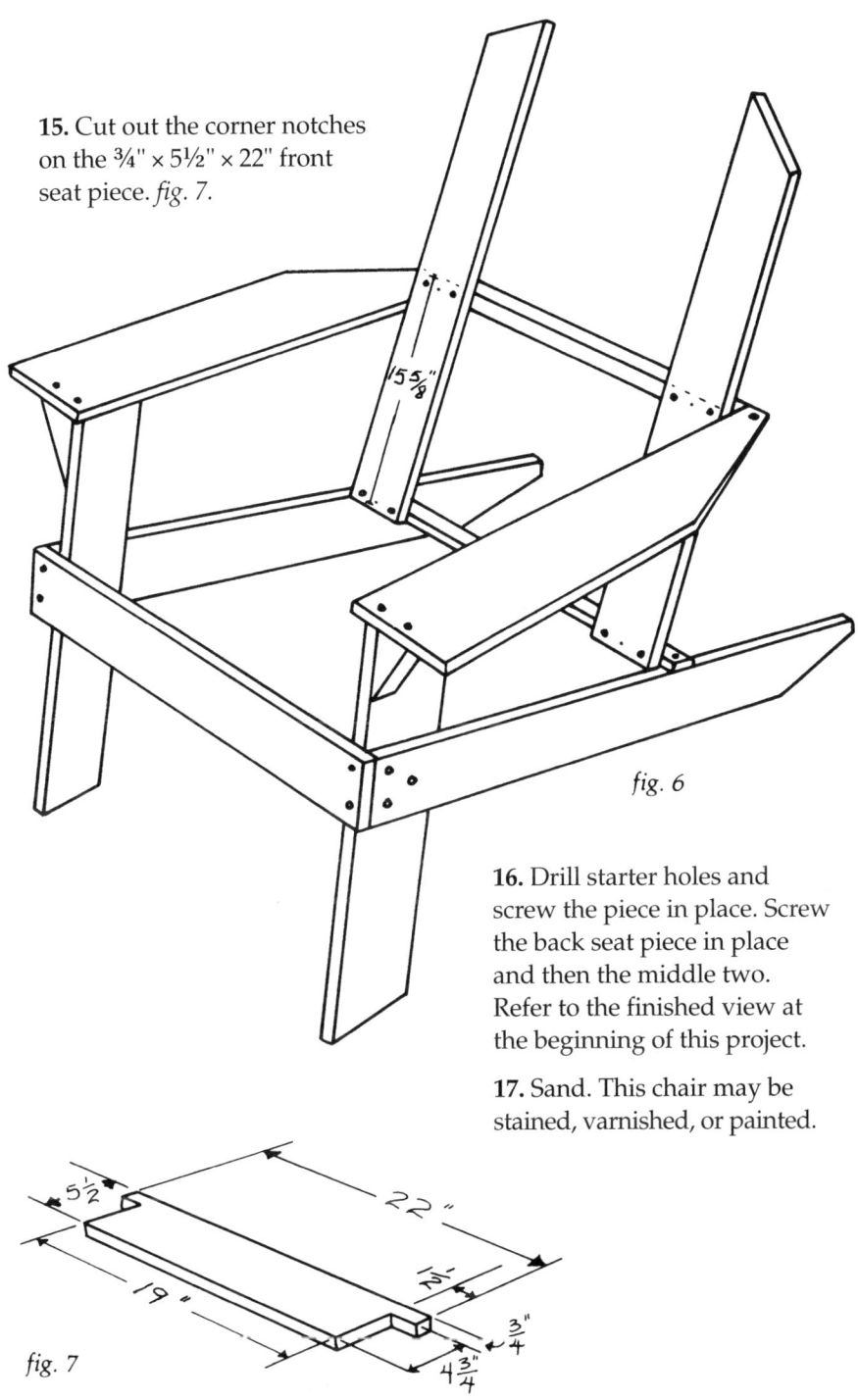

15. Cut out the corner notches on the ¾" × 5½" × 22" front seat piece. *fig. 7.*

5 5⁄8"

fig. 6

16. Drill starter holes and screw the piece in place. Screw the back seat piece in place and then the middle two. Refer to the finished view at the beginning of this project.

17. Sand. This chair may be stained, varnished, or painted.

5½"

22"

½"

19"

¾"

4¾"

fig. 7

Pump Lamp

Children will love this lamp in their bedrooms, showing how the operation of the pump handle produces a flood of light.

Bill of Materials

Pieces	Use	Dimensions: thickness	width	length
1	base	¾"	4¾"	9¼"
1	pump	3½"	3½"	8¼" (4 × 4)
1	top of pump	¾"	4"	4"
1	pump handle	⅜"	1⅛"	7"
2	sides of trough	¼"	1½"	4"
1	large end of trough	¼"	1⅝"	1½"
1	small end of trough	¼"	1¼"	1½"
1	dowel (spout)	½" round × 2" long		

brass-shell pull chain socket, threaded for ⅛" pipe
continuous-threaded pipe ⅛" × 1" long

2" finish nails	lamp shade
wall plug	white glue
lamp cord	plastic wood

Procedure

1. Cut and plane all stock to the sizes given in the Bill of Materials.

2. Bevel the edges on the base.

3. Lay out and plane the camfers on the corners of the pump. *fig. 1.*

4. Lay out the hole for the pump handle in one of the sides. Bore

⅜" holes about ¾" deep and as close together as possible. Clean out with a chisel. Chisel the 30° angle at the bottom of the hole. *fig. 1.*

5. Bore a hole for the spout. Glue the spout into place. *fig. 1.*

6. Bevel the edges on the pump top. *fig. 4.*

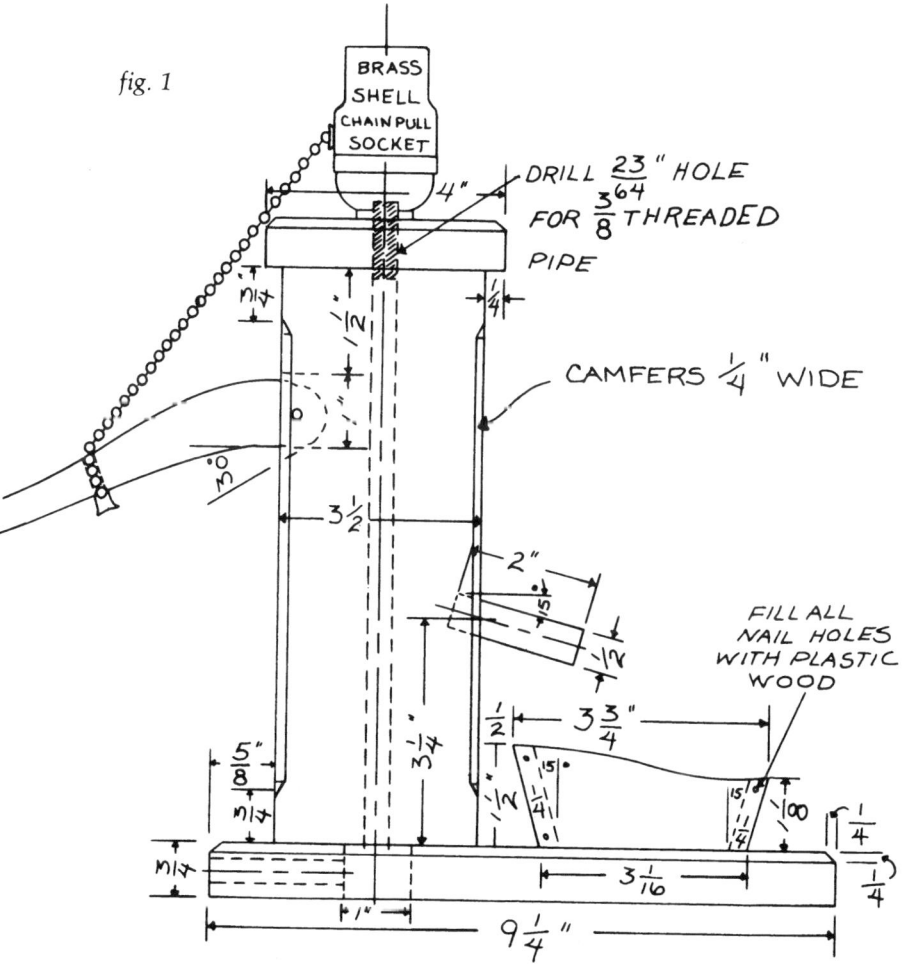

fig. 1

BRASS SHELL CHAIN PULL SOCKET

DRILL $\frac{23}{64}$" HOLE FOR $\frac{3}{8}$ THREADED PIPE

CAMFERS $\frac{1}{4}$" WIDE

FILL ALL NAIL HOLES WITH PLASTIC WOOD

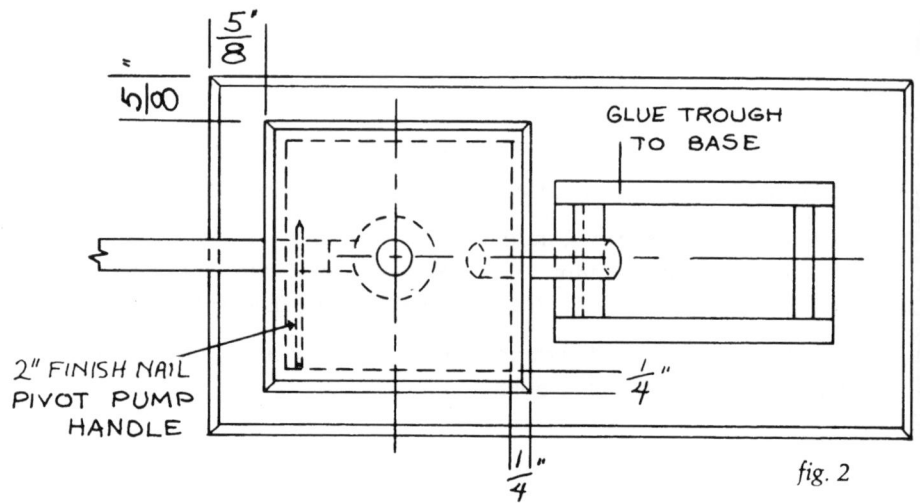

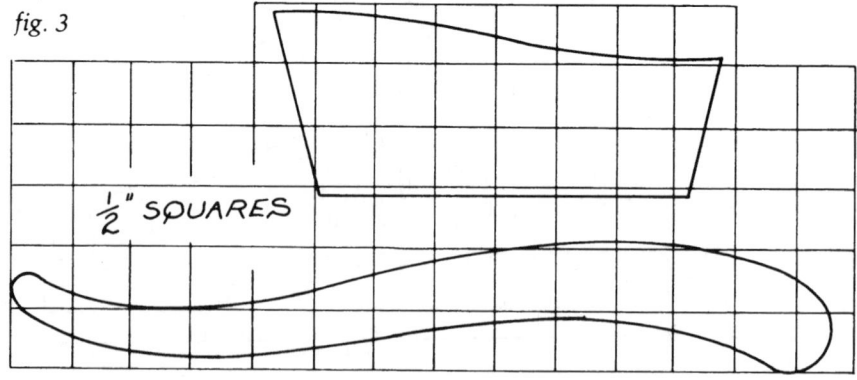

$\frac{5'}{8}$

$5|00$

GLUE TROUGH
TO BASE

2" FINISH NAIL
PIVOT PUMP
HANDLE

$\frac{1}{4}$"

$\frac{1}{4}$"

fig. 2

7. Make full-size patterns for the pump handle and trough sides and transfer them to the wood pieces. *fig. 3.*

8. Saw and sand the pieces to shape. Use a coping saw.

9. Fasten the handle in place. Drill as far as the hole from one side. Fit the handle in the hole so it will swing low enough to switch off the light. Bore hole in handle. *figs. 1 & 2.*

10. Drive the 2" finish nail into the side and through the handle to the opposite side. *fig. 2.*

11. Place the pump in its proper position on the base and mark around it with a pencil. *fig. 2.*

12. Remove the pump from the base. Drill nail holes through the base ⅜" in from the drawn lines.

13. Nail the base to the pump.

fig. 3

$\frac{1}{2}$" SQUARES

14. Fasten the pump top to the pump in the same manner as was done with the base. *fig. 2.*

15. Drill a $^{23}\!/_{64}$" hole through the center of the top down through to the bottom of the base. *figs. 1 & 2.*

16. From the bottom of the base, widen the hole through the base to one inch as seen in *fig. 1.*

17. Drill a $^3\!/_8$" hole from the center of the back of the base through to the 1" hole. *fig. 1.*

18. Assemble the trough. Be sure to keep the top of the ends even with the top of the sides.

19. Plane or chisel and sand the bottom of the ends level with the sides. *fig. 1.*

20. Glue the trough to the base.

21. Screw the threaded pipe into the top.

22. Thread the wire through the base.

23. Take the socket apart and fasten the wires. Screw the base of the socket to the pipe before reassembling the socket to avoid twisting the wires.

24. Attach the plug to the other end of the wire.

25. Locate the point on the handle where the chain will just clear the top. Refer to *fig. 1.*

26. Drill the hole through the handle.

27. Remove the bell from the chain and thread the chain through the hole. Refasten the bell.

28. Fill all nail holes with plastic wood.

29. Sand.

30. This project may be stained, varnished, or painted.

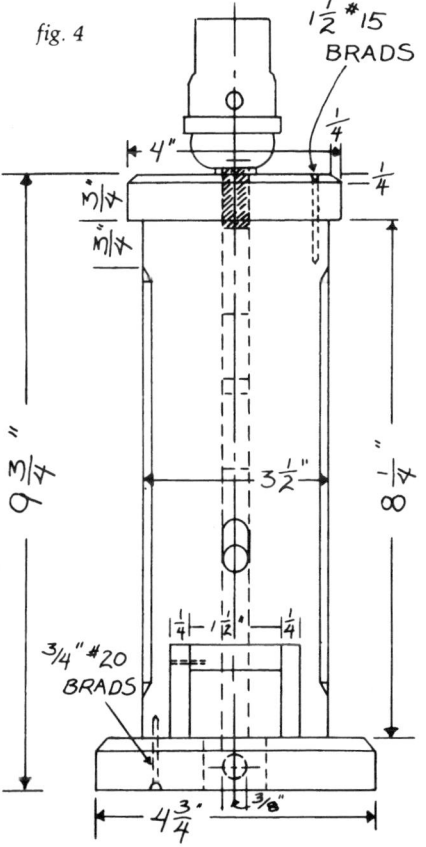

fig. 4

Step Stool

The family will join you in wondering how you got along without it. It's handy for reaching, sitting — one tiny tot even used it as a desk.

Bill of Materials

Pieces	Use	Dimensions:		
		thickness	width	length
1	stool top	¾"	10"	15½"
2	sides	¾"	9"	16"
2	rails	¾"	2½"	12¾"
1	step top	¾"	10"	11½"
2	sides	¾"	9"	8"
1	rail	¾"	2½"	8¾"
1	dowel	½" round × 13½" long		

white glue

Procedure

1. Cut, plane, and square all boards to the sizes given in the Bill of Materials.

2. Bevel the edges on the upper side of the stool and step top with a plane. *fig. 1.*

3. Lay out and cut the mortises (grooves) on the under side of the tops. Bore holes ⅜" wide and ⅜" deep and as close together as possible where the mortises are to go. Clean out the mortises carefully with a chisel. A sharp knife and router plane may also be used. Refer to *fig. 4.* and *step 17* under the Side Table project for instructions on using these tools.

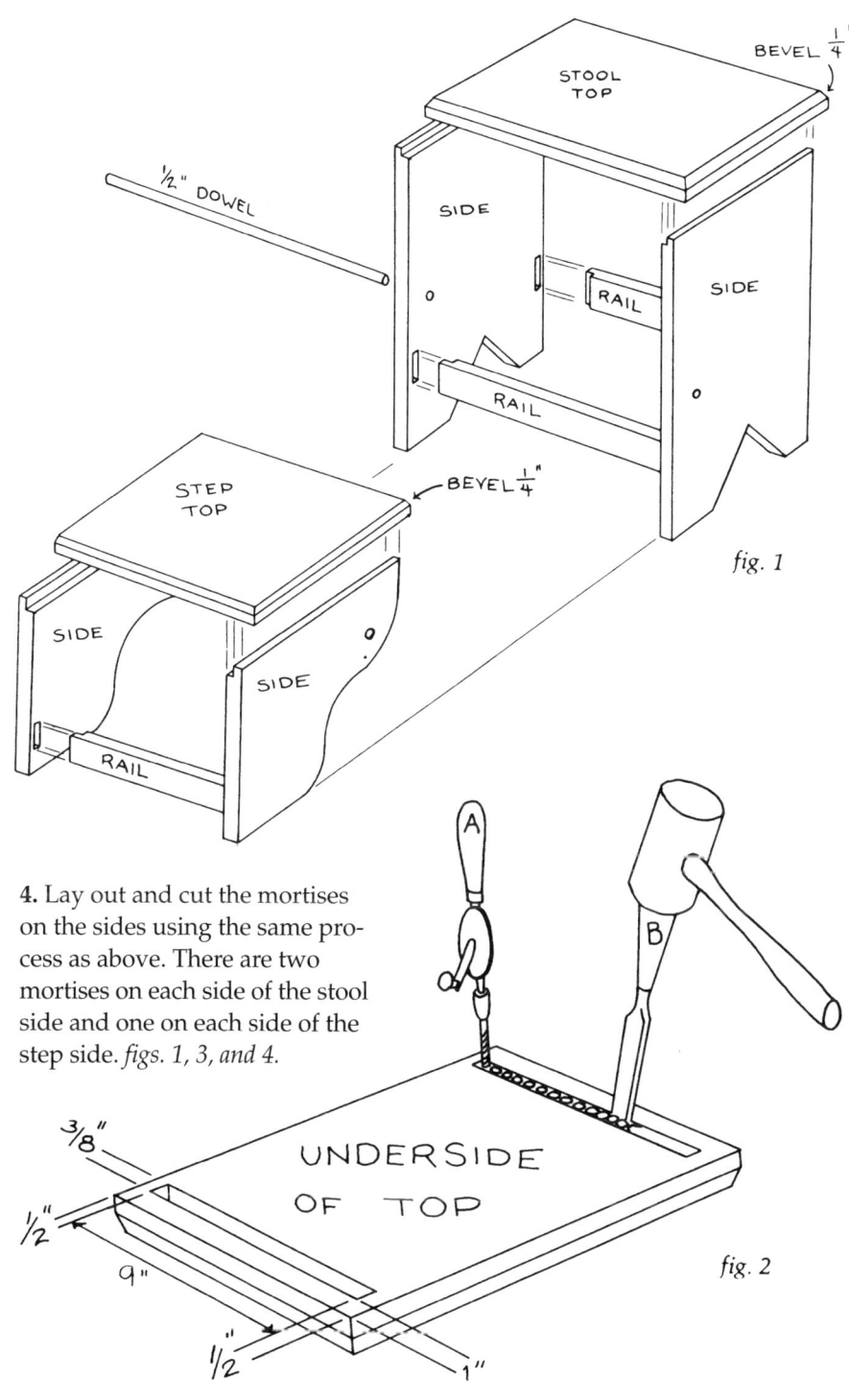

BEVEL $\frac{1}{4}$"

STOOL TOP

½" DOWEL

SIDE

SIDE

RAIL

RAIL

fig. 1

STEP TOP

BEVEL $\frac{1}{4}$"

SIDE

SIDE

RAIL

4. Lay out and cut the mortises on the sides using the same process as above. There are two mortises on each side of the stool side and one on each side of the step side. *figs. 1, 3, and 4.*

A

B

$\frac{3}{8}$"

UNDERSIDE

OF TOP

$\frac{1}{2}$"

9"

fig. 2

$\frac{1}{2}$"

1"

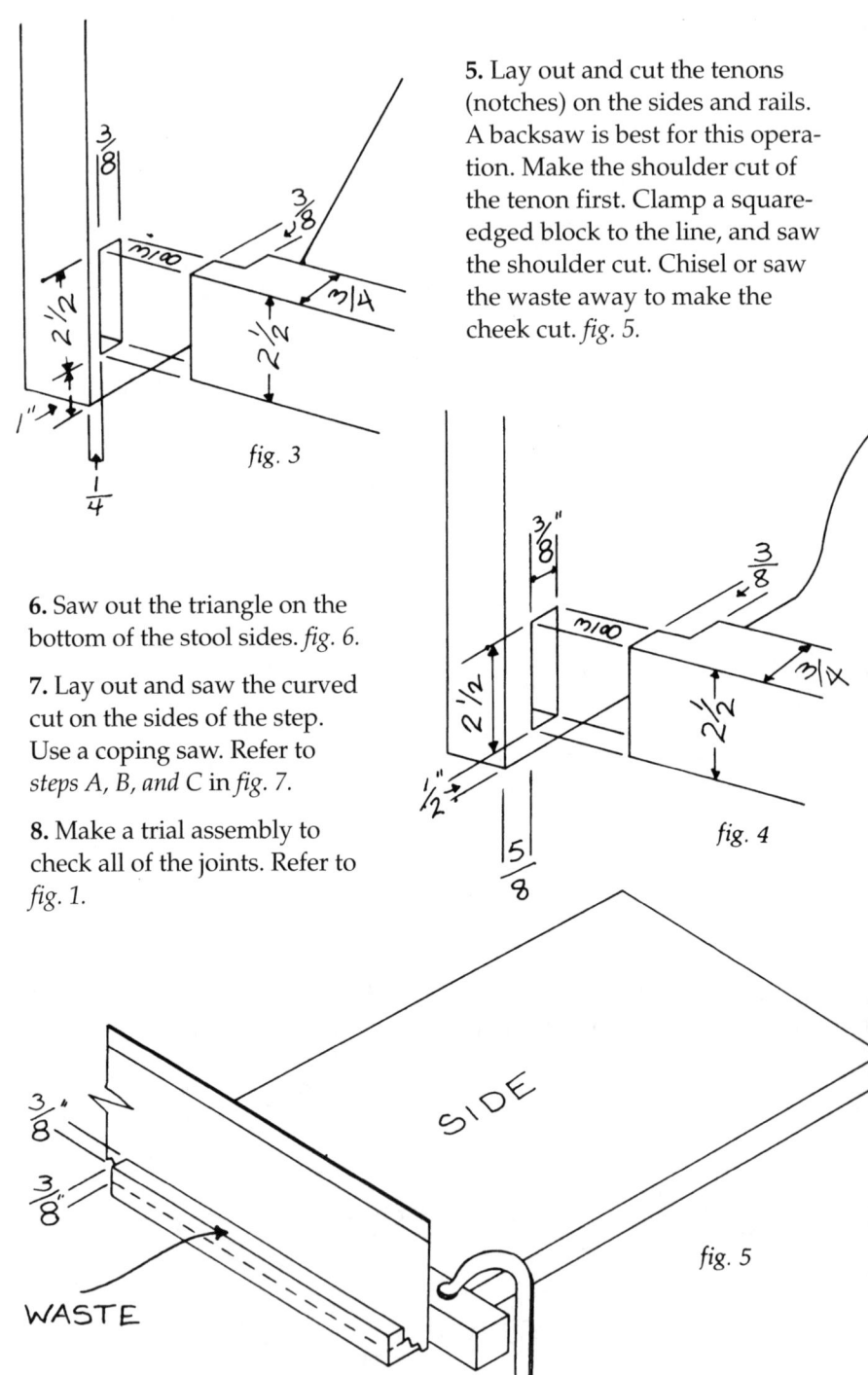

5. Lay out and cut the tenons (notches) on the sides and rails. A backsaw is best for this operation. Make the shoulder cut of the tenon first. Clamp a square-edged block to the line, and saw the shoulder cut. Chisel or saw the waste away to make the cheek cut. *fig. 5.*

fig. 3

6. Saw out the triangle on the bottom of the stool sides. *fig. 6.*

7. Lay out and saw the curved cut on the sides of the step. Use a coping saw. Refer to *steps A, B, and C in fig. 7.*

8. Make a trial assembly to check all of the joints. Refer to *fig. 1.*

fig. 4

SIDE

WASTE

fig. 5

9. Glue and clamp the parts together so that they are square.

10. Lay out and drill the holes for the dowel. Drill holes in the same place on each side of the stool section first. Put the step in place, checking to make sure it will fold back into the stool freely.

Mark where your holes come in on each side of the step. Drill the holes on the step side. Refer to *fig. 6*.

11. Pound the dowel through the holes.

12. Sand the project.

13. An oil, stain, or paint finish is best for this project.

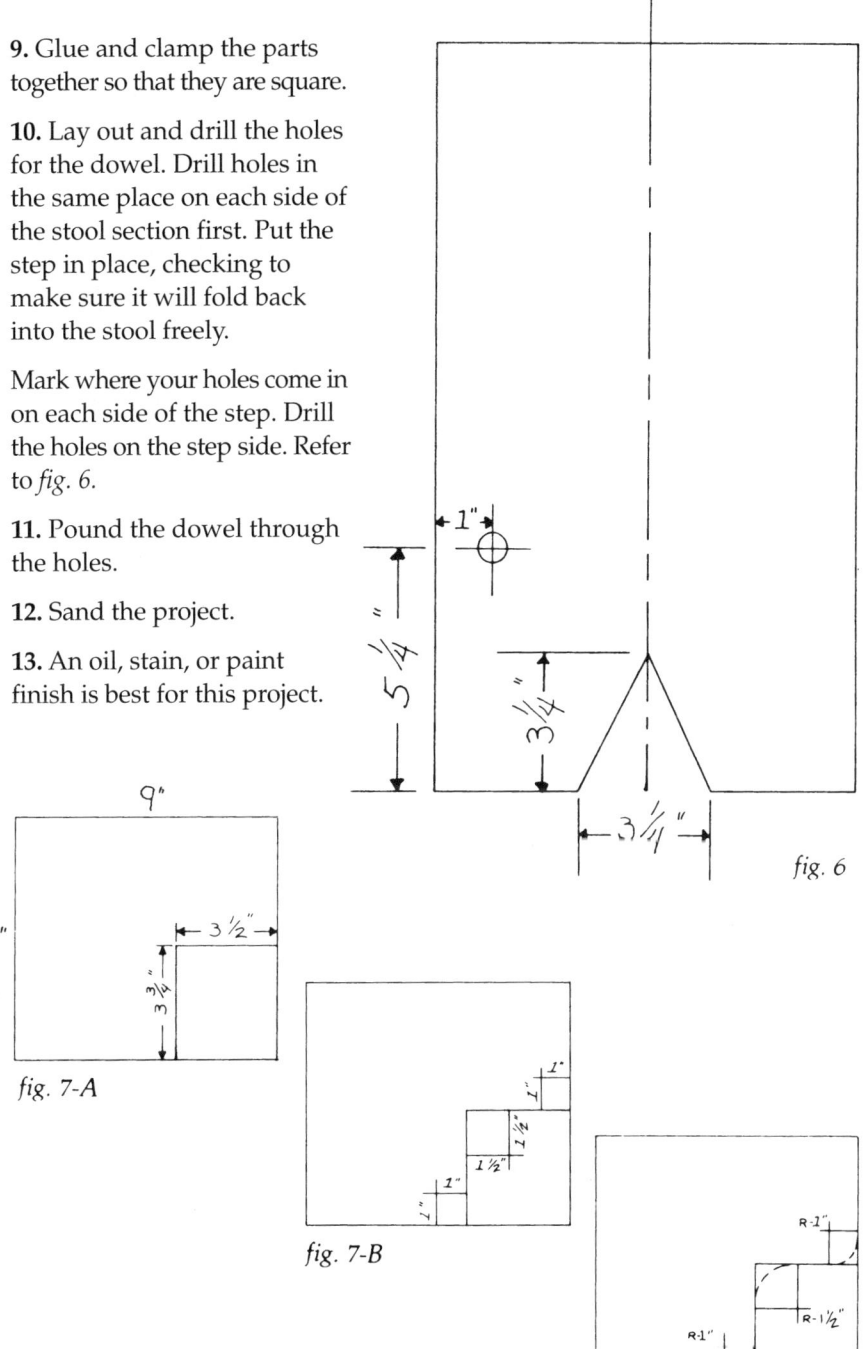

fig. 6

fig. 7-A

fig. 7-B

fig. 7-C

Storage Box

This box is large enough to hold a lot of tools, winter hats and boots, etc. Note that the strength of this box is increased by use of rabbet joints on the sides and bottom.

Bill of Materials

Pieces	Use	Dimensions:		
		thickness	width	length
1	top	¾"	12"	16"
2	front and back	¾"	12"	16"
2	sides	¾"	11¼"	12"
1	bottom	½"	11¼"	15¼"

1	16" long box hinge and screws
1	hasp
	15½" #10 brass plumber's chain
2	#2 round-head wood screws
3'	length of ⁵⁄₁₆" nylon rope
	4-penny finish nails or 1½" #15 brads
	1½" #6 flat-head wood screws
	white glue
	wood putty

Procedure

1. Cut, plane, and square all boards to the sizes given in the Bill of Materials.

2. Lay out and cut the rabbet joints on the sides of the front and back pieces. This may be done with a backsaw and chisel or with a router plane. If you do it with the router plane, clamp the two pieces side by side on the top of your workbench. Cut along the rabbet line on the inside of the side pieces with a knife, using a straight edge to keep the knife line straight. Cut the rabbets on both sides simultaneously with a router plane. *figs. 1 & 2.*

3. Lay out and cut the rabbet joints on the inside of the bottom of the front, back, and side pieces. *fig. 1.*

4. Assemble the side pieces. Start the nails through one side of the rabbet joint until the ends just protrude on the inside. Apply some glue to the joint. Press the end of the shorter side piece against these protruding points, then, resting the opposite end of the short side on the bench, drive the nails home. Attach the other short side in the same manner and finally the opposite long side.

5. Attach the bottom piece to the sides. Apply the glue to the rabbet joints at the bottom of the sides. Put the bottom in place. Drill starter holes and screw the bottom in place. See bottom view in *fig. 1.*

6. Drill $5/16$" holes in the sides for the rope handles. Cut the rope in half, tie a knot on one end of the piece, and thread it from the inside of the box through one hole and back through the other. Finish off the handle by tying a knot on the second end of the rope.

7. Chisel out a $1/16$" deep groove ¾" wide and 16" long on the top edge of the back of the box for the box hinge. Do the same on the underside of the back edge of the top piece. See side and top views in *fig. 1.* See also the finished view.

8. Attach the box hinge to the top piece.

9. Attach the hasp to the center front underside of the top piece. See the front and top view on *fig. 1.*

10. Attach the top to the back of the box.

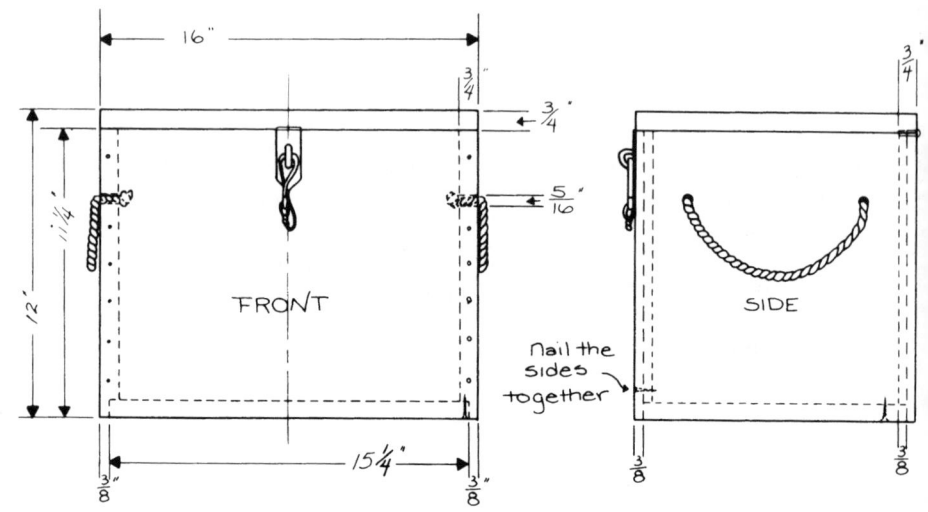

fig. 1

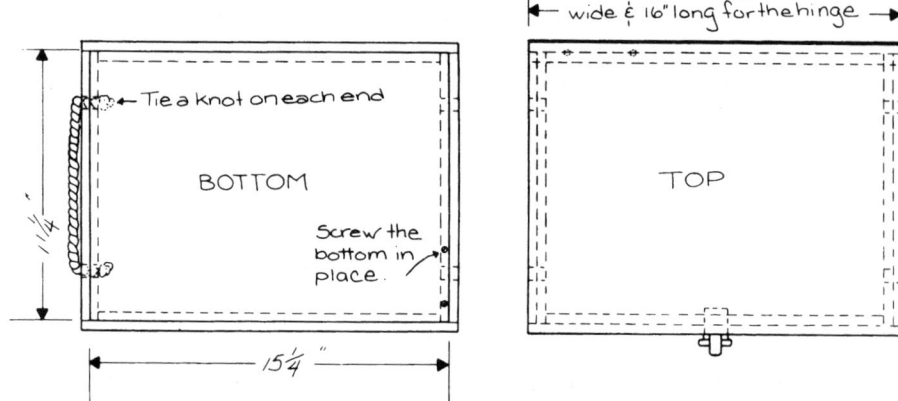

11. Fit the chain to the box and top so that the lid falls back slightly. See the *finished view*.

12. Fit the catch to the hasp.

13. Fill all nail holes with wood putty.

14. Sand. Paint, stain, or varnish as suits your intended use.

fig. 2

Side Table

Win your B.C. (bachelor of carpentry) degree with this one. Graceful lines and drawer make this a table that is both useful and beautiful.

Bill of Materials

Pieces	Use	Dimensions:		
		thickness	width	length
4	legs	1¾"	1¾"	29¼"
2	sides	¾"	6"	14½"
1	back	¾"	6"	14½"
1	stretcher above drawer	¾"	1"	14½"
1	stretcher under drawer	¾"	1¾"	14½"
2	drawer guides	1"	1½"	12½"
2	drawer runs	¾"	1"	14½"
2	strips to fasten top	¾"	¾"	12½"
1	drawer front	¾"	3¹⁵⁄₁₆"	12⁷⁄₁₆"
2	drawer sides	½"	3¹⁵⁄₁₆"	15"
1	drawer bottom (plywood)	¼"	11¹⁵⁄₁₆"	14¾"
1	drawer back (plywood)	¼"	3¹⁵⁄₁₆"	11¹⁵⁄₁₆"
1	table top	¾"	18"	18"

4	1½" #10 flat-head screws
14	1¼" #8 flat-head wood screws
1	box of 1" wire brads
1	drawer pull
	white glue

Procedure

1. Cut and square all stock to the sizes given in the Bill of Materials.

2. Lay out and cut the mortises on the legs. Bore holes ⁵⁄₁₆" wide and 1" deep. Close together where the mortises are to go. Clean out the waste that is left with a chisel. *fig. 1.*

3. Lay out the lines for the taper on the two opposite sides of each leg. Begin the taper 18" from the floor. *fig. 1.*

4. Plane the taper on these two sides, squaring to the sides not yet tapered.

5. Plane the taper on the last two sides.

6. Lay out all the tenons on the stretchers, back, and sides. *fig. 1.*

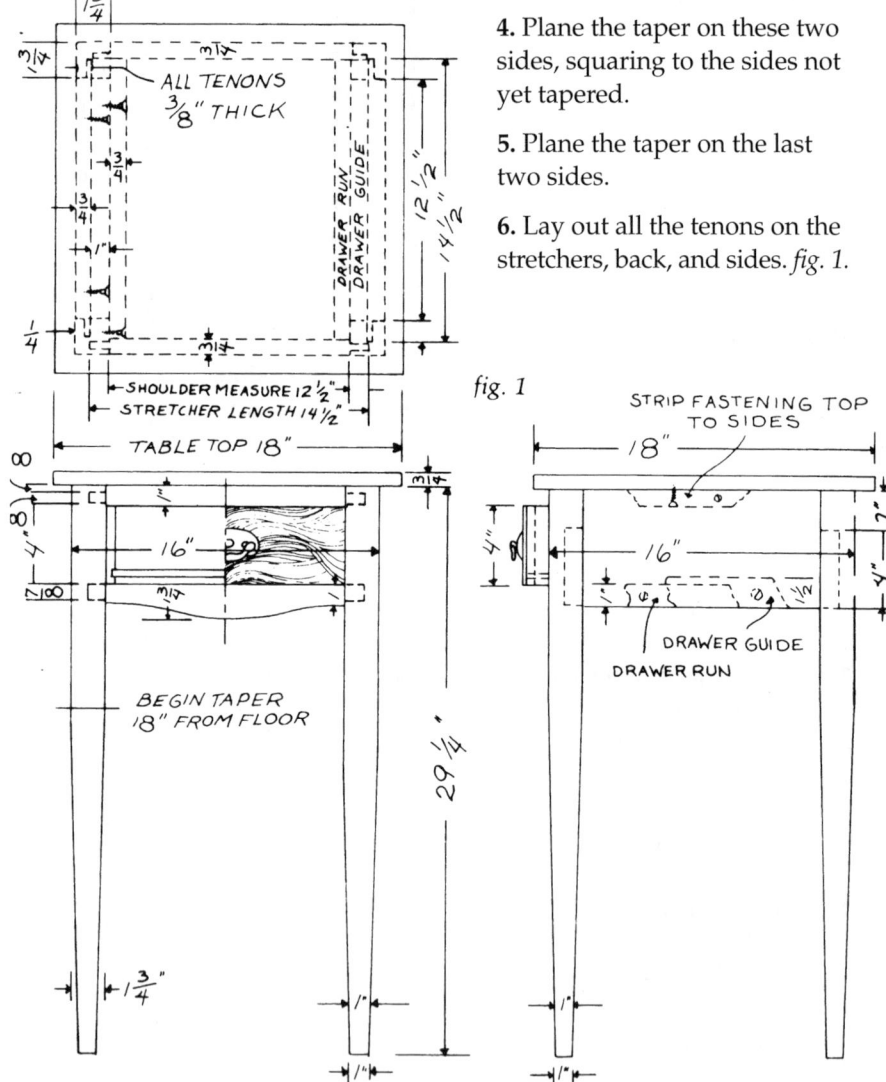

fig. 1

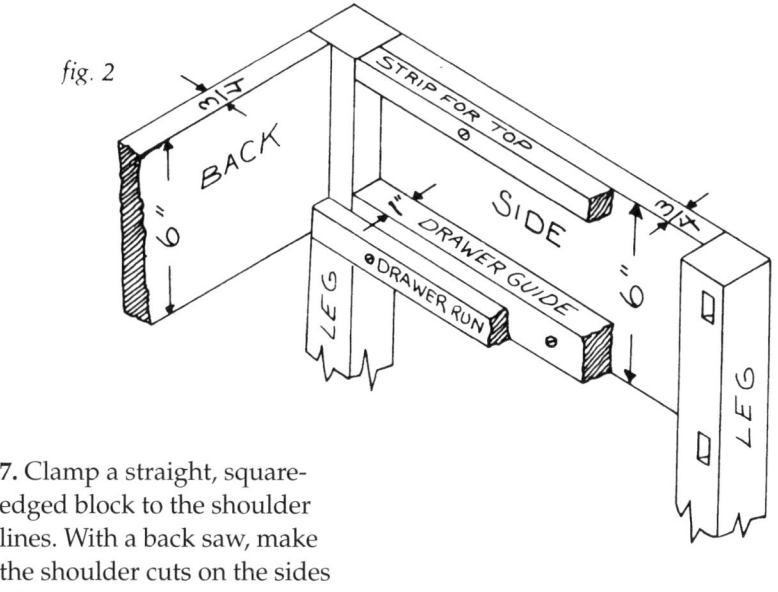

fig. 2

7. Clamp a straight, square-edged block to the shoulder lines. With a back saw, make the shoulder cuts on the sides of the boards and stretchers.

8. Chisel the cheek cuts.

9. Mark the lines for the width of the tenons.

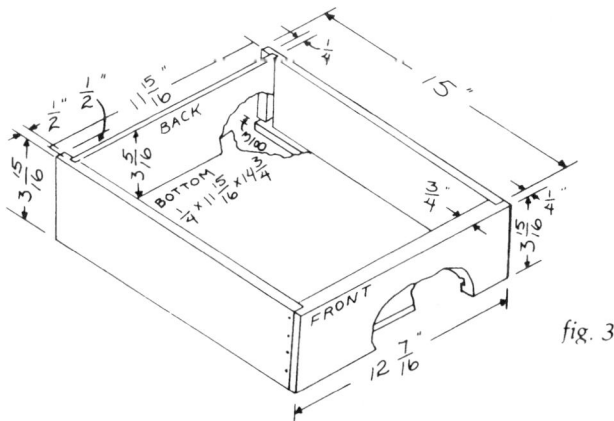

fig. 3

10. Saw to the lines, making the shoulder cuts last.

11. Lay out and cut the curve in the bottom stretcher.

12. Make a trial assembly of all the joints.

13. Fasten the drawer guides and runs. *fig. 2.*

fig. 4

14. Glue up the frame.

15. Lay out and cut the rabbet joints on both ends of the drawer fronts. *fig 3.*

16. Lay out the ¼" grooves in the drawer front and in the drawer sides. *fig. 3.*

17. Cut out the grooves so that they are ¼" deep. This can be done with a drill and chisel or with a knife and a router plane. The knife and router plane will give the cleanest results. To use them, cut along the lines with a knife, and then clean out the groove with the plane. *fig. 4.*

18. Make a trial assembly.

19. Glue and brad the drawer together, keeping it squared in the process. Refer to *fig. 3.*

20. Screw on the strips to fasten the top. *fig. 2.*

21. Fasten the top to the table.

22. Sand.

23. An oil, stain, or varnished finish works well on this project.

24. Attach the drawer pull.

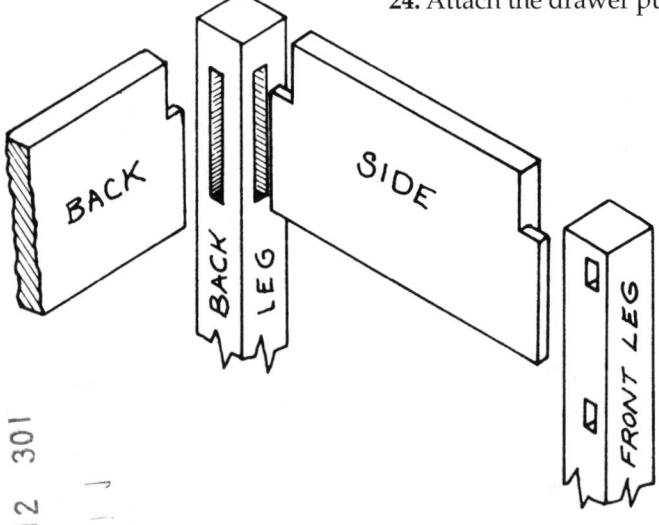

12 301